ABCs
OF THE SEA

By Elizabeth Gauthier

St. Clair Shores, Michigan

1st Edition
Text © 2020 Elizabeth Gauthier
Images from Adobe Stock

For information about permissions
please write Gauthier Publications at:

Gauthier Publications
P.O. Box 806241
Saint Clair Shores, MI 48080
Attention: Permissions Department

Frog Legs Ink is an imprint of Gauthier Publications
www.FrogLegsInk.com

Proudly printed and bound in the USA

ISBN: 978-1-942314-54-7

Library of Congress information on file

For Jenna

Aa

Anchovy

I am delicious as a pizza topping!

Bb

Beluga Whale

I'm the smallest whale!

Cc

Crayfish
I look like a tiny lobster!

Dd

Dolphin

I'm not a fish, I'm a mammal like you!

Ee

Emperor Angelfish

I live in the coral reef!

Ff

I inflate like a balloon
when I'm scared.

Fugu (aka: puffer-fish)

Gg

Great White Shark
I can have up to 3,000 teeth!

Hh

Hammer-head Shark

I have a unique shape that helps me see prey!

Ii

Irokanji

The smallest and one of the most venomous jellyfish in the world.

Jj

Jellyfish

Some jellyfish glow in the dark!

Kk

Killer whale

I'm actually a really big dolphin!

L1

Lobster

Not all lobsters are red!

Mm

Manta ray

I'm the largest of the rays but I eat tiny plankton!

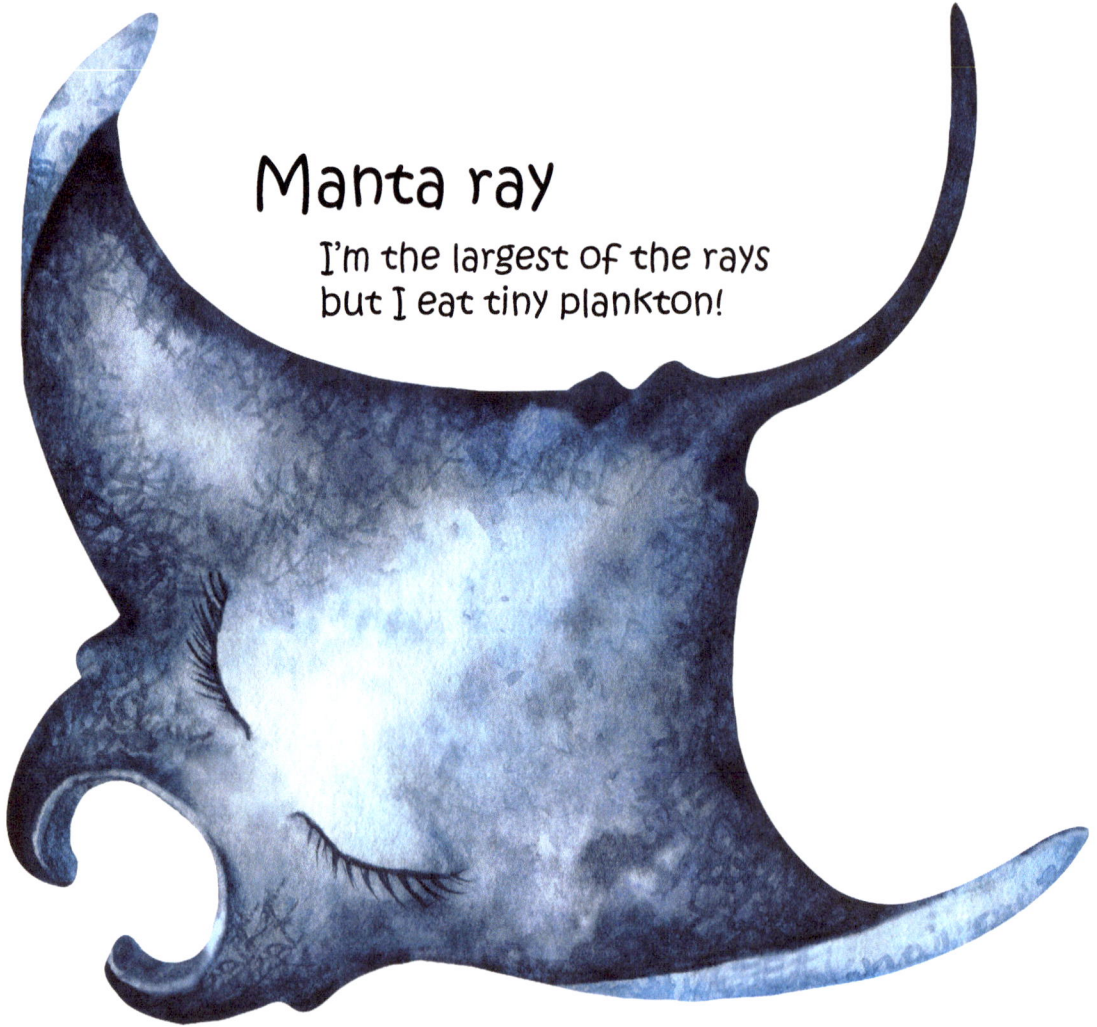

Nn

Narwhal

It looks like I have a unicorn horn but it's really a large tooth!

O o

Oysters

I live inside a shell!

Pp

Pearls

I am made inside of an oyster
and come in all kinds of
pretty colors!

Qq

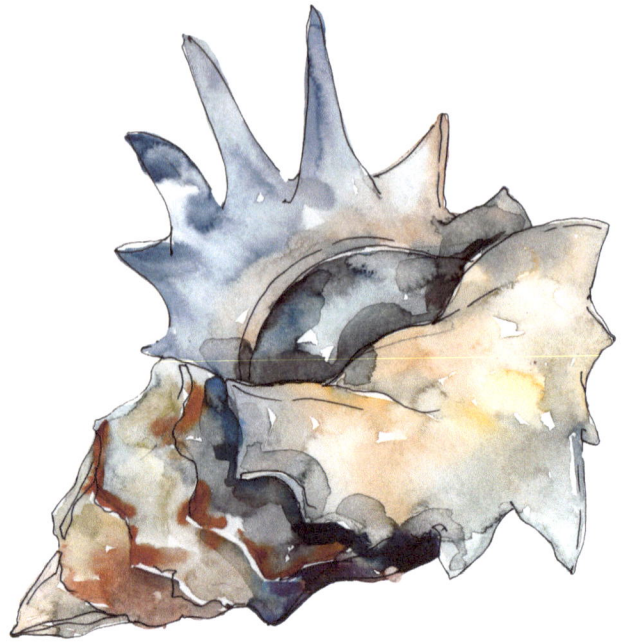

Queen conch

I'm a really big marine snail!

Rr

Ringed seal

I live in the arctic
and am the smallest
seal!

Ss

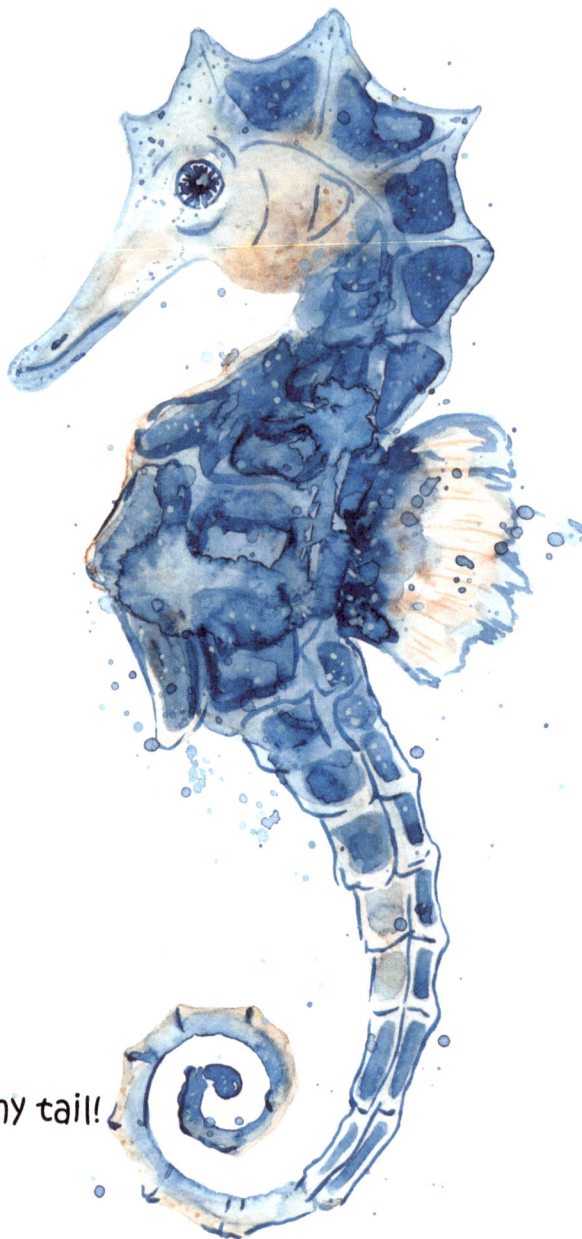

Seahorse

I hold on to things with my tail!

Tt

Tiger shark

I like to eat at night!

Uu

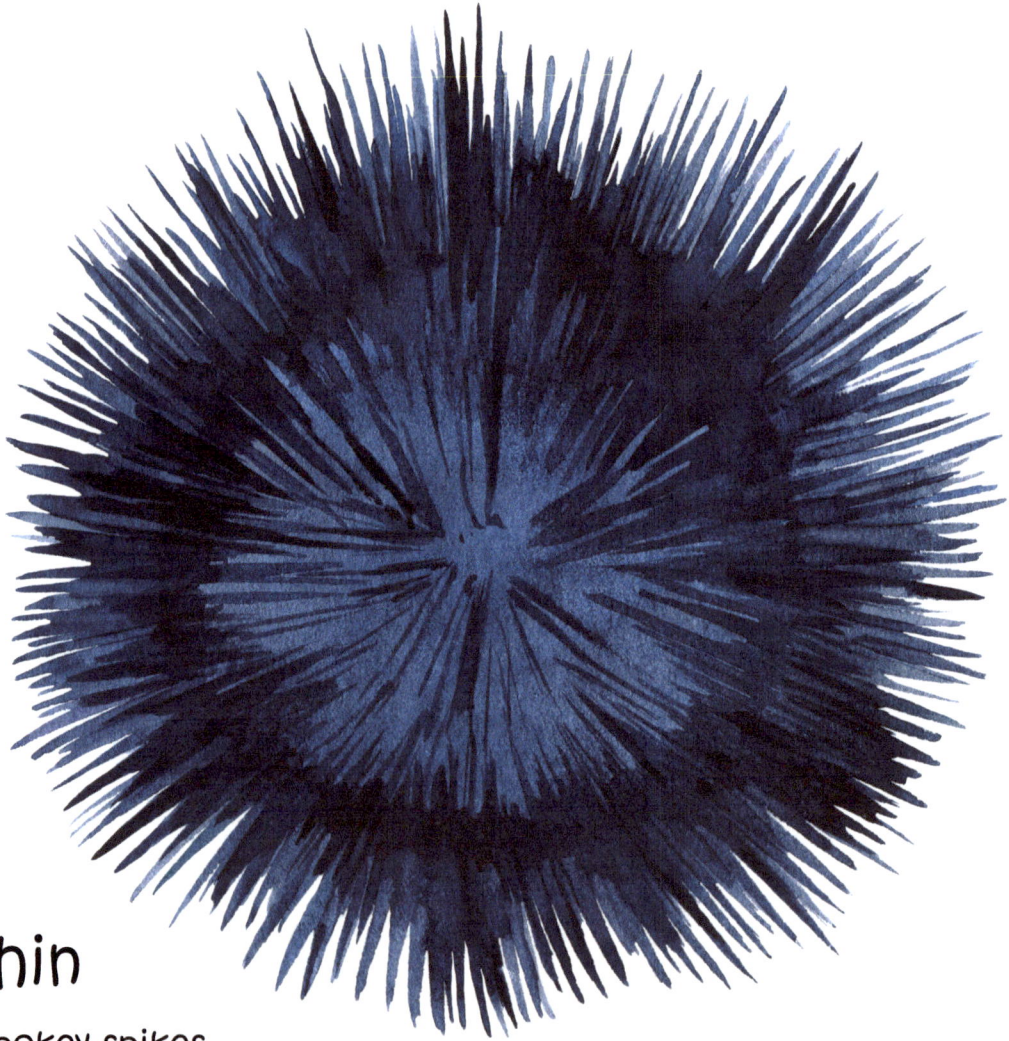

Urchin

I have pokey spikes
like a hedgehog!

Vv

Velvet Crab

I'm covered in tiny hair that make me look like velvet!

Ww

Walrus

I use my tusks to lift myself onto ice!

Xx

X-Ray fish

My body is translucent and
I look like I could live in the ocean
but I live in freshwater!

Yy

Yellow tang

I live by Hawaii!

Zz

Zebra lionfish

I use my spines to defend myself!

1 2 3 with me series
by Elizabeth Gauthier

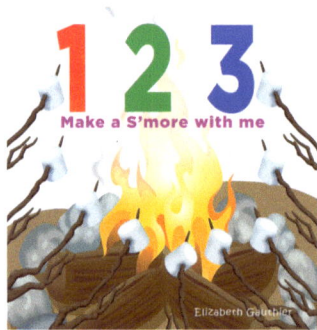

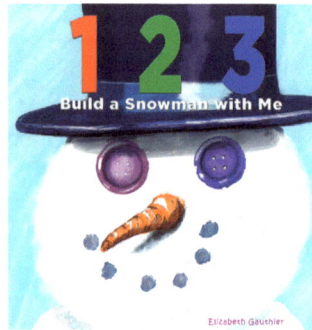

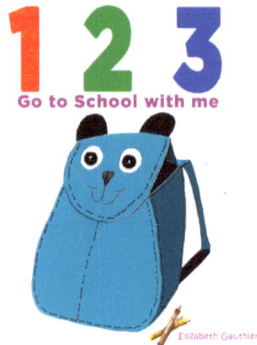

1 2 3 Make a S'more with me
Elizabeth Gauthier

1 2 3 Build a Snowman with Me
Elizabeth Gauthier

1 2 3 Visit the circus with me
Elizabeth Gauthier

1 2 3 Go to School with me
Elizabeth Gauthier

Look for additional activities & lesson plans!

1 2 3 Make a Banana Split with me
By Elizabeth Gauthier